IDEAS AND INVENTIONS

MAKING WORK EASIER

Breakthroughs that Transformed our World

Philip Wilkinson
Illustrated by Robert Ingpen

Chrysalis Children's Books

First published in the UK in 2005 by
Chrysalis Children's Books
An imprint of Chrysalis Books Group Plc,
The Chrysalis Building, Bramley Road, London W10 6SP

Text copyright © Philip Wilkinson 2005
Illustrations copyright © Robert Ingpen 1997, 2005

ISBN   1 84458 210 8

British Library Cataloguing in Publication Data
for this book is available from the British Library.

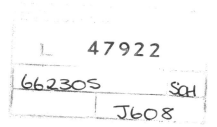

Editorial Manager: Joyce Bentley
Senior Editor: Rasha Elsaeed
Series Editor: Jon Richards
Editorial Assistant: Camilla Lloyd
Designed by: Tall Tree Ltd
Cover Make-up: Wladek Szechter

Previously published in four volumes for Dragon's World *Caves to Cathedrals,
Science & Power, Scrolls to Computers* and *Wheels to Rockets*.

Printed in China

10 9 8 7 6 5 4 3 2 1

CONTENTS

Introduction

One of the most famous inventions of all is the wheel. It is hard to imagine life without it because it makes so many things possible – from vital means of transport like cars and railway engines to all sorts of machines that we use every day. In every case, the wheel makes it much easier to do the things we need to do, and that is why the wheel is so famous – even though no one knows the name of the person who invented it some 6,000 years ago.

The wheel is just one of a number of key inventions that make work easier for people everywhere. Some inventions are kinds of engines, such as the internal combustion engine. These are familiar to us because they have powered many different forms of transport, such as ships, trains and cars. Before the steam engine made railways possible, most people hardly travelled at all. However, it was the coming of the car, powered by the internal combustion engine, that brought cheap, personal transport to millions.

The car could not do this alone. To begin with, cars were expensive luxury items. Each one was made individually, by a highly-skilled work force using hand tools, and only the rich could afford a car. What changed this for

ever was mass production, a way of making things quickly and cheaply by using specialized machines and standard-size parts that could be bolted together on an assembly line. Mass-produced cars could be made for a fraction of the cost of hand-made ones and suddenly millions of people could buy their own vehicle.

Mass production changed the world in the early twentieth century, making all sorts of items easier to make – and more affordable. Another huge step forward came towards the end of the century, with the development of the computer.

Computers transformed office work, allowing people to create documents in seconds and add up long columns of figures in an instant. Today, computers have spread to virtually every area of our lives. Nearly all modern machines, from microwaves to cars, are controlled by tiny computers, making them simple to use in the process. Computers have not just made work easier – they have made many tasks possible without people doing any work at all.

PHILIP WILKINSON

THE WHEEL

Over 5,000 years ago, an unknown inventor brought about a transport revolution by making the first wheeled cart.

Living without the wheel was not as difficult as we might imagine today. For one thing, the tracks and pathways of ancient times were so narrow and uneven that wheeled vehicles would not have been much use. It was better to rely on sure-footed beasts of burden such as mules, llamas, camels and horses. Loads were balanced on the animal's back or carried in panniers slung on each side. Slavery was common in ancient civilizations, so humans were also used as beasts of burden.

ROLLING ALONG

Heavy loads were often pulled or pushed. Sometimes the load was put on rollers made from tree trunks. This was a good way to move large building stones over short distances, but as there were no proper roads, it was not very good for longer journeys.

The sled or sledge was another early means of transport. It was fairly easy to make, and its runners could glide over most surfaces if they were not too rocky.

△ *A travois was one of the best methods of pulling heavy loads before the invention of the wheeled cart.*

THE FIRST WHEELS

The first wheels were usually made of wood. In areas with lots of timber, they were sometimes made of one solid piece of wood (1), but most were made from three pieces of wood joined together (2).

In places where there was no wood available, wheels made from stone were used (3). To make wooden wheels lighter, people began to cut holes in the solid wood (4). Some wheels were made with a strong cross-bar and struts to add strength (5). Eventually, the spoked wheel (6) was invented, combining lightness with strength.

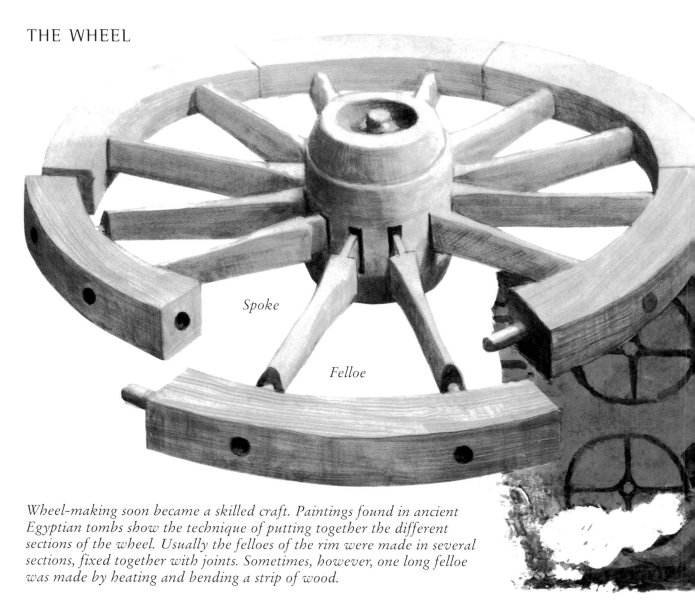

Spoke

Felloe

Wheel-making soon became a skilled craft. Paintings found in ancient Egyptian tombs show the technique of putting together the different sections of the wheel. Usually the felloes of the rim were made in several sections, fixed together with joints. Sometimes, however, one long felloe was made by heating and bending a strip of wood.

Sleds were in use in Europe by 5000 BC and had probably also been invented independently in other parts of the world by then. They are still used for transport in polar regions.

Another type of vehicle, the 'travois', was even more adaptable. It was made of two wooden poles arranged in a V-shape with the point towards the animal pulling it. The open ends trailed on the ground behind. A light framework or net filled the space between the poles to support the load. For travelling people like the nomads of Central Asia and North America, the travois had the advantage that the poles could be separated at night and used as tent supports.

THE FIRST WHEELS

No one knows exactly when or where the wheel was invented, but it was probably about 6,000 years ago in the Middle East. A clay tablet found at Erech in Mesopotamia, dated about 3500 BC, has a picture of a sledge mounted on four solid wheels. This was about the same time as a wheel was first used for making pottery.

By 2500 BC, wooden-wheeled carts seem to have been widely used in the ancient civilizations of the Middle East and in the Indus Valley in India. When the British archaeologist Sir Leonard Woolley (1880–1960) excavated the city of Ur in the 1920s, he found the remains of several wheeled vehicles. Similar remains have also been found in other Middle Eastern and Indian locations. By the first century AD, the use of wheels had spread through the Mediterranean, northwards though Europe to Scandinavia and eastwards to China.

ACROSS THE ATLANTIC

Although the ancient civilizations of North, Central and South America were

advanced in many ways, they did not discover the wheel. When Europeans began to settle in the Americas in the sixteenth century, they took their knowledge of the wheel with them. Three centuries later, it was the wheels of carts that enabled the far west of North America to be settled by pioneers.

As knowledge of the wheel spread throughout the ancient world, there were many improvements. It is possible that the first wheels were made of single discs of wood or even stone, but the earliest carts found by archaeologists had wheels made from three pieces. Three shaped pieces of wood were joined together by two or more cross-pieces at right angles.

WHEEL AND AXLE

There were two ways of connecting the wheel to its axle. In some vehicles, the axle was fixed to the vehicle and the wheel turned around the end of it. This method worked well for light vehicles. In heavier vehicles, the wheel was fixed to the axle and the whole axle turned as the vehicle moved.

Fixed axle

Rotating axle

This type of wheel probably developed after the discovery that metal could be worked and fashioned into tools and nails. A metal saw would have been needed to cut wood accurately enough to make the three main pieces of the wheel, and copper nails were often driven round the finished edge to protect it from wear and tear.

WHEELS AT WAR

All through history, new inventions have been quickly adopted for use in war, and the needs of warfare have often led to improvements. The story of the wheel follows this pattern.

Wheeled vehicles enabled large numbers of troops to be carried quickly into battle, surprising the enemy with a moving target that was difficult to hit.

Pictures of two-wheeled war chariots are shown on items found in the royal tombs of the city of Ur, dating from about 3000 BC. At first, they were probably used to carry kings into battle, but they were soon adapted as troop-carriers.

LIGHTENING THE LOAD

It was probably the use of war chariots that led to the next important step forward in wheeled transport. This was the spoked wheel. Chariots needed to be fast and manoeuvrable. Solid wheels made them heavy, cumbersome and difficult to turn. The first stage in the development of the spoked wheel was to remove some of the solid wood between the wheel's outer rim and its hub. This made the wheel lighter, but could also weaken it.

CHARIOT RACES

The ancient Greeks developed chariot racing as a sport. It was a gruelling test of the riders' courage. The two-wheeled chariots were specially designed for racing. They were lightly built and carried only one person. Unlike the drivers of war chariots, the racing driver was seated. A rail at each side protected him from the wheels and enabled him to take sharp bends in safety.

Chariot races were an important part of the ancient Olympic Games. Competitors had to drive their chariots round a course which had a post at each end. The greatest skill was needed to make each turn in safety, as close to the post as possible. As the competitors manoeuvred into their positions for the tight turns, the spectators cheered and yelled with excitement.

*An early
Scandinavian
cart.*

By about 1400 BC in Egypt, and about 100 years later in China, tools and woodworking skills had reached a stage where wheels could be made in separate sections of hub, spokes and rim, and then joined together. The rim was sometimes made in several pieces, called felloes, held together with joints.

Another method was to heat and bend a long strip of wood into a circular rim, fixing the spokes into it to hold its shape. The wheelwright's craft became a specialized and highly skilled branch of carpentry, demanding the precise use of tools and a good eye for the quality of wood. The ancient Greeks used two different types of spoked wheel.

For carts, they made heavier wheels with crossbars across the rim and strengthening pieces of wood in the middle to form the hub. Chariots had wheels with four, six or eight spokes set into the inside edge of the rim.

NORTHERN SKILLS

The Celtic peoples of northern Europe added their skills to the development of wheeled transport. Experts in working metal, they also had the advantage of plentiful supplies of wood. The Celts made iron tools for wheelwrights to use, and also developed a method of 'shoeing' their wheels with iron tyres. Red-hot tyres were usually placed over the rim

It was not until the seventeenth century that vehicles began to be fitted with springs. Before this time, passengers and goods had no protection at all from the jolting caused by bumpy roads.

and then plunged into water, so that the iron contracted tightly over the rim. As the metal shrank, it hardened, giving the wheel added strength. The Celts often used different woods for the different parts of their wheels. The spokes might be made of hornbeam, the rim of a single piece of ash, and the hub of oak.

WEAR AND TEAR

Many historians think that the Celts may also have come up with the first solution to another problem. Whether the wheels were fixed to an axle and went round with it, or rotated individually on their own hubs, the continuous movement caused wear. In time, either the axle or the wheels would become loose and would have to be replaced. Some Celtic carts have been found to have grooves

in the hubs. These grooves could have held wooden rods which turned between the hub and the axle, making a simple bearing. It would have been far easier and cheaper to replace the rods than to fit new wheels or axles.

The design of the spoked wheel bound with an iron tyre changed little between ancient Celtic times and the coming of the railways. It was suitable for all kinds of vehicles, from royal carriages to humble farm carts, and is still in use today.

The only major change was the introduction of springs in the seventeenth century. At first, these were leather straps attached to the axles of passenger carriages to take the weight of the vehicle's body and give a smoother ride. Later, steel springs of various shapes were fitted between the axles and the vehicle body.

Ball bearings between the wheel hub and the axle were also introduced in the eighteenth century. They not only reduced wear on the hub and axle, but also needed less maintenance. Previously, wheel hubs had to be thoroughly greased before each journey, but ball bearings contained a supply of oil which could last for weeks or even months.

REINVENTING THE WHEEL

It was only when the heavier loads and faster speeds of the railways, and, later, of motorized road vehicles, demanded stronger wheels that engineers began to rethink the design of the wheel. The railways gradually abandoned spoked wheels for solid metal. On the roads, the design of wheels had to change when the inflatable rubber tyre was invented.

The first rubber tyres were made of solid rubber, and these continued in use, especially for heavy goods wagons, until the 1920s. The air-filled leather tyre first appeared in 1845 and was the invention of a Scotsman, Robert Thomson (1822–73). Four of his tyres were fitted to a horse-drawn carriage and driven

for nearly 1,600 kilometres before they wore out. However, the public was not impressed, and Thomson's invention was soon forgotten.

Forty-two years later, another Scot, John Boyd Dunlop (1840–1921), made the first air-filled or 'pneumatic' tyre, using a tube inside a rubber outer casing. His invention was taken up enthusiastically by racing cyclists, and so the first pneumatic tyres were designed for bicycles.

A few years later, cars began to appear on the roads and they too adopted pneumatic tyres. The first car wheels had wire spokes like bicycles, but by the 1930s, these were being replaced by pressed steel plates. The evolution of the modern wheel was complete.

▽ *The first tyres were made from solid rubber, but pneumatic tyres filled with air proved more successful.*

THE STEAM ENGINE

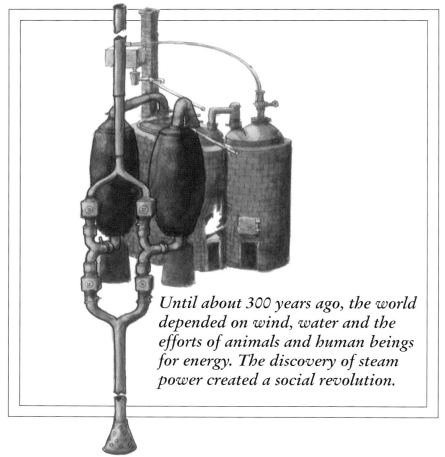

Until about 300 years ago, the world depended on wind, water and the efforts of animals and human beings for energy. The discovery of steam power created a social revolution.

The knowledge that steam could produce energy is about 2,000 years old. An Egyptian engineer called Hero (first century BC) made a machine called an 'aeolipile' in which steam caused a metal sphere to rotate. The aeolipile was a toy with no practical use, but it showed that steam could be a source of energy.

The modern history of steam power began with a French scientist, Denis Papin (1647–c. 1712). He spent most of his working life experimenting with gases and vacuums. The pressure cooker was one of his inventions. Papin also designed a simple steam pump to provide the power for fountains. The pump worked, but the high pressure of water it created kept bursting the pipes. In 1690, Papin had the idea of building an engine in which steam would raise a piston inside a cylinder, creating a vacuum as it rose. This was the principle of later steam engines, but Papin never managed to make an engine that worked.

△ *Thomas Savery's steam engine, the 'Miner's Friend', was made to pump water out of mines.*

THE POWER OF STEAM

For centuries, people were fascinated by the power of steam, but unable to think of a practical use for it.

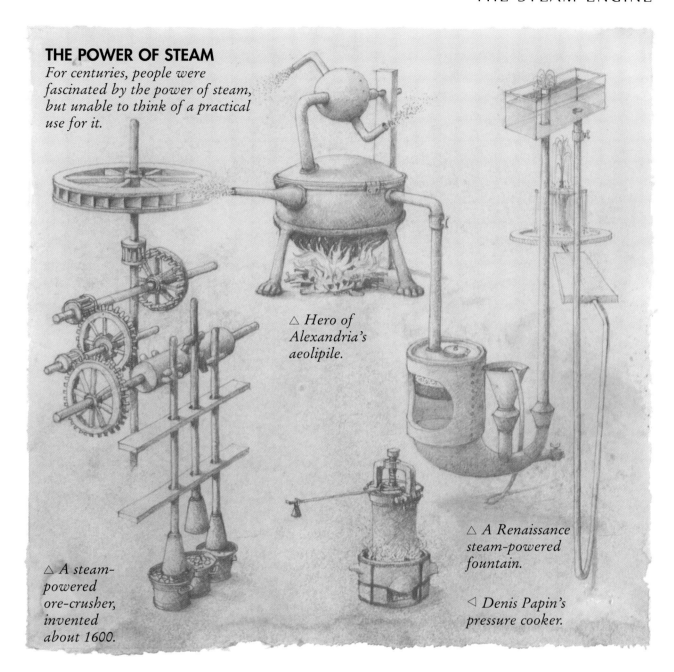

△ *Hero of Alexandria's aeolipile.*

△ *A steam-powered ore-crusher, invented about 1600.*

△ *A Renaissance steam-powered fountain.*

◁ *Denis Papin's pressure cooker.*

THE MINER'S FRIEND

The first successful steam engine arose out of the urgent need to pump water out of flooded mine shafts. In 1698, an English engineer, Thomas Savery (c. 1650–1715), invented a steam pump. He called it the 'Miner's Friend'. It had a cylinder which was filled with steam from a boiler. When the cylinder was cooled by pouring cold water on the outside, a partial vacuum was created.

The vacuum drew water into the cylinder from the mine shaft. The Miner's Friend would pump water upwards only about six metres. If the water was any deeper, the engine became unsafe and sometimes even blew up.

Another Englishman, Thomas Newcomen (1663–1729), invented a safer steam engine that could pump from greater depths. Its cylinder was cooled by water sprayed from inside. Unlike the

OPPOSITION TO STEAM

To people who had been used to the quiet and leisurely pace of horse-drawn transport, the speed, power and noise of steam locomotives was terrifying.

The first victim of a railway accident was a British cabinet minister, Sir William Huskisson (1770–1830). At the opening of the Liverpool-to-Manchester Railway in 1830, he stepped into the path of the oncoming train and was killed.

Some even believed that rail travel could be dangerous. In the 1830s, an eminent Irish scientist, Dr Dionysius Lardner (1793–1859), warned that travelling at a speed of 48 kilometres per hour could make the brain fall apart. In Britain, Queen Victoria was persuaded to make a train journey from Windsor to London in 1842 to show that rail travel was safe.

Country people in particular were opposed to railways. They had good reason, because the noise and smoke of trains often frightened livestock grazing by the line and made horses throw their riders. Another problem was that sparks from locomotive chimneys came down in line-side fields and set fire to growing crops. However, farmers later found that they benefited from railways, because trains could get their goods to market more quickly than before.

Miner's Friend, Newcomen's cylinder was open at the top. This space was filled with a piston, a circular iron plate which fitted tightly but could still slide up and down. An iron rod was fixed to the piston. As the steam from the boiling water below made the piston rise and fall, it operated a beam connected to a pump.

Like Savery's pump, Newcomen's engine used a huge amount of coal to raise steam. This did not matter when it was used in coal mines, where there was plenty of fuel. From 1712, when the first Newcomen engine was installed in a coal mine in the English Midlands, it became standard equipment in many British pits. Shafts could now be sunk deeper and more coal extracted. However, where there was no coal close at hand, the cost of fuel was too high.

IMPROVING THE ENGINE

At this point, the best-known name in the history of steam comes into the story. James Watt (1736–1819) was a Scottish instrument maker and repairer working at the University of Glasgow. In 1763, he saw a Newcomen engine for the first time when the university sent a model in for repair. Watt was a true scientist, always questioning and experimenting. Soon he was working on ways to improve the efficiency and cut the fuel consumption to the Newcomen engine.

Watt's first improvement was to separate the heating and cooling stages of the engine's operation. Having to heat the water and then cool it in the same cylinder made the Newcomen engine slow and was also the main cause of its heavy use of fuel. Watt designed an engine with a separate condenser where the cooling process could take place. Meanwhile, the cylinder stayed hot all the time. This meant that there was no pause while the cylinder reheated.

The addition of a condenser was only one of the improvements made by James Watt. Of the others, the most important for the future of transport was his

▷ *James Watt improved on the steam engines available at the time and made steam power a practical source of power for industries.*

△ Rails were used to pull vehicles along in mines before steam trains. It was easier to pull heavy loads along the smooth rails than the uneven ground. At first, ordinary flat wheels were used on rails. Then wheels were given edges called 'flanges' to help keep them in place.

introduction of a set of gears which he called 'sun and planet'. Until then, steam engines could produce only an up-and-down movement. The piston made to rise and fall by steam in the cylinder was attached to a beam which also rose and fell. Watt's sun and planet gear enabled the piston to turn a gear wheel, the 'planet', which meshed with a second gear, the 'sun'. The 'sun' was connected to a wheel shaft and made it turn.

Watt had found the way to change the up-and-down movement of the piston into a rotary movement. In other words, Watt's sun and planet gears could make steam engines turn wheels. The possibility of steam-powered transport had, at last, become a reality.

THE FIRST STEAM CARRIAGE

James Watt was not really interested in transport. He designed a steam vehicle in 1784, and his assistant William Murdock (1754–1839) built a working prototype, but the two engineers took the idea no further. It was left to others to explore the possibilities of the steam engine as a means of transport.

In 1770, a Frenchman, Nicolas Joseph Cugnot (1725–1804), had made a steam wagon for hauling heavy field guns. Cugnot's wagon had a maximum speed of 3.6 kilometres per hour and was not a success. It showed that steam-powered transport was possible, but there was a problem. Efficient steam transport demanded high pressure steam. Could a boiler be made to withstand such high pressure? This difficulty was to hold back many designers of early steam engines.

An English engineer called Richard Trevithick (1771–1833) made a determined effort to solve the problem.

After making a number of successful stationary steam engines for mines, he began to experiment with steam road vehicles. In 1801, he drove his first steam carriage on the road. It had not travelled far before it overheated and exploded, but Trevithick carried on with his work. By 1804, he had succeeded in producing a steam locomotive that hauled a ten-tonne load of iron, as well as about 70 people, along a 16-kilometre length of cast iron tramway in Wales.

ON THE RAILS

This was the first time that a steam train had travelled on rails, but the idea of using rails to provide a more even surface than the bumpy, rutted roads of those days was not new. Wooden tramways had been used for horse-drawn transport in coal mines for at least 200 years. In about 1800, some of these wooden tracks began to be replaced by longer-lasting cast iron rails. It was Trevithick's idea of bringing together the iron tramway and the steam locomotive that marked the launch of the Railway Age.

At first, progress was slow. In 1808, Trevithick built a small circular railway track in London to demonstrate his new locomotive, *Catch Me Who Can*. Plenty of people came to see it, but the railway was still seen as a toy, not a serious means of transport. Trevithick lost heart and turned to other interests.

Meanwhile, steam locomotives had caught the attention of another Englishman, George Stephenson (1781–1848). In 1814, he built his first locomotive for the colliery where he was the engineer. Eleven years later, his engine *Locomotion* hauled the first railway train on the newly-built line, 42 kilometres long, between Stockton and Darlington in northern England. This was the first railway in the world open to the public, with regular services in each direction. However, people were still unsure about the safety of steam travel. Locomotives were used to haul coal trains on the Stockton-to-Darlington line, but passenger services were horse-drawn.

THE RAINHILL TRIALS

The idea of railways began to catch on, not only in Britain, but also in other countries. Plans were made for railway lines in France, the USA and Germany. Meanwhile, in Britain, a line was planned between Liverpool and Manchester,

▽ *Cugnot's three-wheeled steam carriage had a top speed of 3.6 kilometres per hour. It could carry up to four people.*

a distance of 64 kilometres. The directors of the Liverpool-to-Manchester line were anxious to find the best locomotive for the job, and announced a competition with a prize of £500. It was to be decided by trials over a special length of track at Rainhill, near Liverpool.

The trials were held in October 1829. Ten engineers promised to take part, but in the end only five locomotives turned up for the trials. Two failed to get up enough speed, which left three including the *Rocket*, built by George Stephenson and his son Robert (1803–59). The *Rocket* was proclaimed the winner when its two rivals suffered burst boilers. Stephenson's prize was not only a cheque for £500 but also an order for eight similar engines. When the Liverpool-to-Manchester line opened in 1830, the *Rocket* proudly headed the first train.

RAILWAY MADNESS

The success of the *Rocket* sparked off a rush to build railways. The first United States line opened in 1830, and soon there was a network of lines linking the important east coast cities with the coal-mining areas of Kentucky and West Virginia. France's first steam railway also opened in 1830 between St Etienne and Lyons, and Germany followed in 1835. There was such a rush to build railways that people began to speak of 'railway madness'.

There were rapid improvements in the performance of steam engines, but the railways led to developments in other technologies as well. Building tracks through boggy or mountainous country gave engineers new challenges as they tackled cuttings, embankments, tunnels and viaducts. Many of the lines built then, over 150 years ago, are still used by today's much heavier and faster trains.

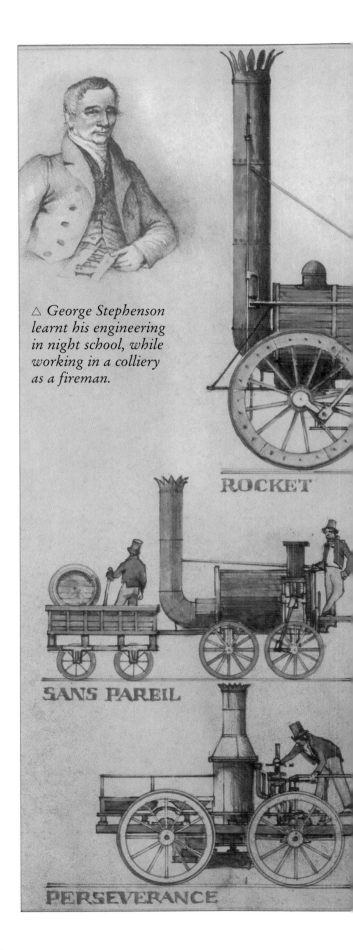

△ *George Stephenson learnt his engineering in night school, while working in a colliery as a fireman.*

ROCKET

SANS PAREIL

PERSEVERANCE

Five locomotives took part in the Rainhill trials. Two of them failed to reach the required speed, Perseverance *and* Cycloped, *a locomotive powered by a horse on a treadmill.* Sans Pareil *and* Novelty *both blew up during the trials, leaving Stephenson's* Rocket *the outright winner.*

NOVELTY

CYCLOPED

Meanwhile, the railways made a vast difference to the lives of ordinary people. Travel was faster and easier than it had ever been. Soon, people were living at a distance from their work and commuting each day by train. The railways made travelling for holidays possible. They also made the transport of goods from place to place easier and cheaper. Fresh meat and vegetables, milk and other dairy products became easier to buy. New towns grew up close to the railway lines. Builders no longer had to depend on local materials, and farmers could transport their cattle to market by train instead of driving them slowly along the roads.

Army generals, too, were quick to realize that railways were an efficient method of transporting troops. The first use of railways in war was in the Crimean War (1853–56) when Britain and France fought Russia. A temporary railway was built to carry British troops into battle and to evacuate the wounded.

STEAM CONQUERS THE WORLD

Within 50 years of the opening of the first steam-powered railway, the steam locomotive had conquered

RAIL GAUGES

The width of the track between railway lines is called the gauge. The gauge of the Stockton-to-Darlington railway was 1.435 metres, which was said to be the standard gap between the wheels of wagons used in the area. This gauge was used on most of the railways in Britain and many other parts of the world. However, some countries, like Russia for example, used a wider gauge. This caused problems when trains were scheduled to cross borders. One solution was to remove the bodies of the carriages by crane and transfer them to wheels of the new gauge. Another answer was adopted in Britain where one railway company, the Great Western, used a gauge of 2.13 metres for many years. This was to lay an extra rail in between, set to the standard gauge so that trains of either gauge could use the track.

almost the whole world. By 1869, it was possible to cross the United States from the Atlantic to the Pacific by rail. The east-west link across Canada was opened in 1887. India's and Australia's first railways opened in 1854, and Africa's in 1870. Some of these lines gave links with the outside world to places that had been almost completely cut off before.

Most of the world's railways now operate with diesel or electric locomotives, but if it had not been for the pioneers of steam many would not have been built at all.

STEAMSHIPS

Soon after the invention of the steam engine, inventors began to wonder if steam could free sailors from the uncertainties of relying on the wind for power. American engineers led the way in the development of steam for shipping.

Using steam to power ships posed a problem. How exactly was the ship to be pushed forward? James Rumsey (1743–92), an American engineer, built

△ *Richard Trevithick and his locomotive* Catch Me Who Can.

a ship with an engine that pumped water out from the stern. It reached a speed of 6.5 kilometres an hour in trials on the Potomac river. Another American, John Fitch (1743–98), used oars driven by a steam engine in his ship, the *Experiment*.

Robert Fulton (1765–1815) was more successful. He devised the paddle wheel which was mounted in the centre of the ship. The ship's engine drove a shaft which was the axle of the paddle wheel. As the wheel revolved, its paddles pushed backwards through the water and drove the ship forwards. Fulton's steamship *Clermont* was successful and it began making regular passenger trips in 1807.

STEAM AT SEA

At first, steamships were used only on rivers and canals or for short voyages within sight of land. For work on the Mississippi River in the United States, shipbuilders developed a design with a large paddle wheel at the stern. These ships were called 'stern-wheelers'. Only the lower part of the paddle wheel went under water, so that stern-wheelers could be used where the water was shallow.

Taking a steamship out into the ocean was a bigger challenge. No one knew how a ship with a heavy engine would behave in rough seas. The huge amount of fuel used by early engines was another problem. In 1819, an American ship, the *Savannah*, became the first steamship to cross the Atlantic. Like all the early

△ *A Mississippi stern-wheeler.*

ocean-going steamers, the *Savannah* also had sails for use if the engine broke down or fuel ran short. In fact, the sails were used for most of the voyage. The first ship to use steam all the way was the Dutch-owned *Curaçao*, which steamed from Rotterdam to the West Indies in 1827. The voyage took a month.

THE GREAT STEAMSHIP RACE

Excitement about crossing the ocean by steam grew. In 1838, there was a race across the Atlantic between two competing British ships, the *Sirius* and the *Great Western*. The *Sirius* made the voyage from Liverpool to New York in eighteen days, but towards the end of the journey the cabin furniture and even one of the masts had to be used as fuel. The *Great Western* took only fifteen days, and arrived with plenty of coal to spare.

It was a British shipowner, Samuel Cunard (1787–1865), who started the

first regular steamship service across the Atlantic, carrying mail, in 1840. The company he started is still operating ships today. Soon, regular services carrying passengers, mail and cargo were crisscrossing the world's oceans. However, the days of the paddle steamer were soon to come to an end.

In 1839, an Englishman, Francis Smith (1808–74), and a Swede, John Ericsson (1803–89), both built ships with screw propellers instead of paddles. They were found to go faster and use less fuel. American shipbuilders were slow to use propellers, but several European shipping companies were soon building new propeller ships for the North Atlantic crossing. In the end, the propeller won, and, as the old paddle steamers wore out, they were replaced by propeller ships.

STEAM SHRINKS THE WORLD
Just as railways opened the way to the interiors of the continents, so steamships

brought the continents closer together. Farmers and manufacturers found new markets for their products overseas, carried quickly and reliably by steamer. The steamship was also responsible for large movements of populations, as millions of people from Europe crossed the oceans to begin new lives in North America, Australia and New Zealand.

Within less than a hundred years, steam had changed the world. In 1800, the fastest means of transport on land had

△ *Steam provided ocean-going ships with a reliable source of power and speed that they had never known before.*

been horsepower. At sea, travellers had depended on the way the wind blew. By 1900, there were few large towns or cities in the world without a railway station, and travel by rail had become fast and cheap. At sea, a network of regular steamship services carried passengers and cargo across the world.

INTERNAL COMBUSTION

Today, we are living in the age of internal combustion. Millions of cars powered by internal combustion engines are used for getting to work, going shopping or taking holidays, and making cars is one of the world's major industries.

There is an important difference between a steam engine and an internal combustion engine of the kind used in cars and trucks. In a steam engine, the fuel is burned in a separate boiler to make steam, which, in turn, provides the force to make the engine work. In an internal combustion engine, the fuel is burned inside the engine itself. This makes the internal combustion engine a lighter and more easily controllable machine than the steam engine.

THE GUNPOWDER ENGINE

The story of the internal combustion engine begins over 300 years ago with a Dutch scientist called Christiaan Huygens (1629–95). In about 1680, he built an engine which used gunpowder as fuel.

△ *The earliest powered vehicles used steam to drive them. Steam carriages never became popular because they were not efficient.*

▷ *Many people were terrified by the first cars. The noisy, smelly vehicles also caused accidents by frightening horses. Until 1896 in England, there was a law that a man had to walk ahead of each car carrying a red flag as a warning.*

INTERNAL COMBUSTION

The explosion of the gunpowder raised a piston inside a cylinder, which fell again as the hot gases from the explosion cooled. Today, it sounds rather strange and highly dangerous to run an engine on gunpowder, but Huygens had the right idea. All internal combustion engines are driven by explosions. A modern car engine works because of the explosions of a mixture of fuel and air which take place all the time the engine is running.

The idea of internal combustion was forgotten in the excitement over steam, and it was not until the 1840s that a French inventor, Etienne Lenoir (1822–1900), returned to it. His engine ran on coal gas. It worked well, but it used so much gas that it was not a serious rival to the steam engine.

OTTO'S ENGINE

As with many important inventions, no one person can be described as the inventor of the modern internal combustion engine. Many scientists and inventors tried out different ideas in the middle of the nineteenth century. In 1876, a German engineer, Nikolaus Otto (1832–91), built the first successful internal combustion engine. His engine was fuelled by coal gas, but was not intended for transport. The aim was to find something more compact and convenient than the steam engine to power pumps and factory machines.

The oil industry in those days was very small. Oil was used only for lighting and cooking, and as a lubricant. Some engineers began to experiment with oil as a fuel for engines. Their work developed along two lines, and led to the two main types of internal combustion engines that we have today: the diesel engine and the petrol engine. It was the petrol engine that was the first to be fitted to a car.

HE COMING OF THE MOTOR CAR

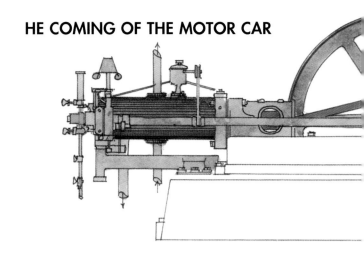

△ *Otto's coal gas engine, built in 1878, was the first internal combustion engine. It was too heavy to be used in a moving vehicle, but was useful in industry.*

Karl Benz

◁ *Daimler's petrol engine was much lighter than Otto's, so it could be used in a moving vehicle.*

Gottlieb Daimler

△ *Daimler added an internal combustion engine to a strengthened bicycle to produce one of the first motor vehicles in 1885.*

◁ *Benz's car still looked rather like a horse carriage used at the time.*

BEYOND THE CAR

While some engineers concentrated on using internal combustion to power a 'horseless carriage', others saw the possibility of adding it to a bicycle. Bicycles were very popular at the time that the first cars appeared.

The first motorcycles appeared in France and Germany about 1885. They had no gears. The engine drove a leather belt which passed around the hub of the rear wheel. The first two-speed motorcycle was produced in 1902, soon followed by machines with three-speed gearboxes.

Other inventors saw that there was a future for the internal combustion engine for general haulage work and in farming. The first lorry to be fitted with an internal combustion engine was built in America in 1902. Soon after, the first tractor was built for farm use, again in America.

One of Otto's assistants was Gottlieb Daimler (1834–1900). Daimler left to set up his own business, and, in the mid-1880s, he began to experiment with petrol as a fuel. This was mixed with air and drawn into the engine at exactly the right moment when it would explode and drive the piston.

On his third attempt to build his engine, Daimler was satisfied with its performance and fitted it to a bicycle. In 1886, he tried this out on the roads. The next year, he took a four-wheeled carriage, removed the shafts used to attach a horse to it and fitted his engine. This was the first 'horseless carriage'.

In the same year, another German engineer, Karl Benz (1844–1929), fitted a similar engine to a tricycle. He went on to build four-wheeled vehicles.

Daimler's and Benz's cars were the first to go into production for sale to other people. Benz built his own cars, but Daimler sold his engines to a French company, Panhard and Levassor, which built bodies for them. These were the first car bodies that did not copy the design of horse-drawn carriages. The 1894 model had many modern features such as a metal chassis, a bonnet over the engine, and clutch, brake and accelerator pedals.

The first cars were expensive, and were regarded more as toys for rich people than as a serious means of transport. Owners also had to be prepared to have a sense of adventure and an understanding of engines, because breakdowns happened frequently.

As engines became more reliable, more

▽ *Diesel's engine was patented in 1892. It works by igniting oil in compressed air.*

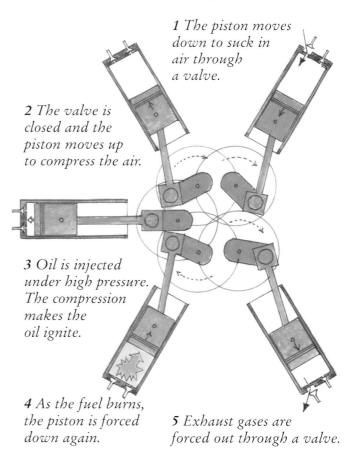

1 The piston moves down to suck in air through a valve.

2 The valve is closed and the piston moves up to compress the air.

3 Oil is injected under high pressure. The compression makes the oil ignite.

4 As the fuel burns, the piston is forced down again.

5 Exhaust gases are forced out through a valve.

people wanted cars, and as more cars were made, the price of them went down. By the 1920s, motoring was beginning to become an everyday experience for millions of people.

THE DIESEL ENGINE

While Daimler and Benz were experimenting with petrol engines, another German engineer had been working on an internal combustion engine which worked in an entirely different way. Rudolf Diesel (1858–1913) gave his name to the kind of engine fitted to trucks, buses and some cars.

Diesel's engine used an oil similar to paraffin instead of petrol. It drew air into the cylinder, where it was compressed by the piston. When this compressed air met the fuel which had been forced into the cylinder, the mixture ignited and there was an explosion, forcing the piston upwards.

Diesel patented his engine in 1892, however it was not until 1898 that he demonstrated it at an exhibition in Munich. It was an immediate success despite its size and weight, and was quickly adopted for use in factories. Later, lighter and more compact versions were developed for heavy road vehicles, tractors and eventually for cars.

CHALLENGE FOR THE FUTURE

The internal combustion engine changed the lives of everyone in the twentieth century. Today, we rely on it for personal transport, for deliveries, for emergency services such as fire-fighting and in countless other ways. However, it has also brought problems. The most serious of these is air pollution from vehicle exhausts, which has ruined the quality of the air in many cities. The challenge is to develop a means of personal transport which does not damage our health.

THE FOUR-STROKE ENGINE

Otto's engine worked on a cycle of four movements.

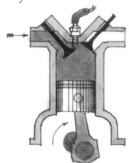

1 The piston moves down and an inlet valve is opened so that gas and air are drawn into the cylinder.

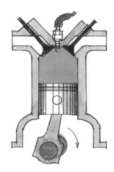

2 The valve is closed and the piston moves back compressing the mixture. A spark ignites the fuel.

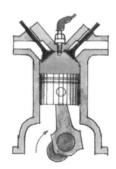

3 The gases in the cylinder expand as they burn, forcing the piston back down.

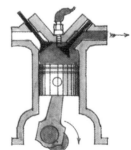

4 Burnt fuel is released through the exhaust valve.

MASS PRODUCTION

Building a car is a long and complicated job for one person. However, mass production methods made the job easier and the car cheaper. It made the dream of owning a car come true for millions of people.

Τhere was a time when every article that was made, a clock, a cart, a table or even a gun, was crafted with hand tools and put together by a single person in a workshop.

The invention of the steam engine changed all that. Processes such as shaping and polishing wood or metal could now be done by machine much more quickly than by hand. Machines could also make parts which were exactly the same. The processes of manufacture could be broken down into small tasks to make the best use of the workers' skills.

So, in making a clock, for example, one person could make the gears, another the springs, a third the face and a fourth the case. A fifth person could then put the clock together.

△ *Gun-stock making was one of the first crafts to be taken over by mass-production methods, early in the nineteenth century.*

◁ *American Eli Whitney (1765–1825) was a pioneer of mass production, producing guns for the US government. Other arms makers soon adopted the techniques. The most successful was Samuel Colt (1814–62) who made the famous Colt revolver shown here.*

Today, there is nothing very surprising about this way of working. It is the way most things are made. However, 200 years ago, it was something new and strange. The old craft methods had been built up over hundreds of years. Many workers thought that the skills they had painstakingly learned were going to waste. This was partly true. Instead of learning all the different processes of clock-making, for example, a worker could be trained in just one process, such as making the face. But the new method, called 'mass production', meant that many articles, from furniture to firearms, became cheap enough for ordinary people to buy.

SPARE PARTS

Mass production was first used in the United States in the manufacture of hand guns at the beginning of the nineteenth century. One advantage appreciated by customers was that if a part developed a

△ *Sewing machines were a nineteenth-century invention perfectly suited to being mass produced. Large factories, like the Singer factory in the USA, employed thousands of workers.*
1 *The machine bodies were cast in a foundry.*
2 *Steam hammers were used to help beat metal parts into shape.*
3 *Lathes were used to cut screws.*
4 *Needles, parts which often needed replacing, were manufactured by the thousand.*
5 *Rows of machines were used for polishing sewing machine parts.*
6 *The sewing machines were tested before leaving the factory.*

fault, it could easily be replaced from a stock of identical parts instead of having to be sent back to the maker for an individual repair. Parts of the same model of revolver could be changed for other identical parts.

Many of the new inventions of the nineteenth century, such as the sewing-machine and the bicycle, were manufactured by mass production methods. However, it was the car industry that proved the value of mass production.

The first cars were built by hand in the old-fashioned way. Each part of the engine, for example, was made to fit that particular engine and no other. If it broke or wore out, the manufacturer had to make a new one that would fit exactly, and the owner had to wait while this was done. A small team of workers would build up each car piece by piece. This took a long time and made cars expensive.

The most difficult task in making a car is assembling all its parts. The engine has to be fitted into place on the chassis, followed by the steering-wheel and pedals, the clutch, the gearbox and all the other working parts. Finally, the body of the car had to be built, painted and, finally, polished.

CARS FOR EVERYONE

At the beginning of the twentieth century an American carmaker, Eli Ransom Olds (1864–1950), began using some mass production methods. Instead of making all the parts for his Oldsmobile cars in his own factory, he bought in parts made by other manufacturers. These were delivered to the Oldsmobile factory and trundled round on trolleys to the assembly workers.

Another carmaker improved on Olds' methods. Henry Ford (1863–1947) began making cars in 1892. By 1902, he had set up his own business. At that time, motoring was a hobby for the rich. Ford's idea was that if cars could be made cheaply enough, and designed to be reliable, everybody would want one. He was thinking particularly of the farmers of the United States who needed a basic vehicle they could depend on to take themselves and their families to town and

BICYCLE POWER

The bicycle became a popular means of transport because it was easily produced by assembling a small number of interchangeable, mass-produced parts. This kept the cost down and made bicycles cheap enough for ordinary people to buy.

The modern bicycle was invented in Britain in 1876, when it was called the 'safety bicycle'. It quickly replaced the older 'penny-farthing' type which had a large front wheel, 1.5 metres in diameter. The first mass-produced safety bicycles were made in 1885 and very soon became popular for travel to work and for leisure cycling.

Part of the success of the bicycle was that, as it was mass-produced, owners could do their own repairs and maintenance by buying spare parts from cycle shops and fitting them themselves.

carry farm supplies about their land. The farmers were not rich, and they would have to be persuaded that owning a car was worthwhile. So Ford set about designing a car for them. To keep the price down, he introduced something into his factory which was to revolutionize the manufacture of almost all factory-made products. It was the 'assembly line'.

On the assembly line, the car's chassis and wheels were put together first. Then they moved on to successive 'work stations' where, one by one, the engine,

controls, brakes and other components were added. Finally, complete cars emerged at the end of the line, ready to be tested and sent off to the showrooms. Using this system, Ford cut the time taken to produce a single car from 12 hours to 90 minutes.

THE MODEL T

The first car produced on Ford's assembly line was the Model T, designed with American farmers in mind. It was a huge success and became the most successful car of all time. The first Model T was built in 1909. By 1925, half the cars in the world were Model Ts, and when production ended in 1927, 15 million had been made. Model Ts were cheap and reliable. If anything went wrong, spare parts could be found easily at one of the chain of dealers that Ford had set up all across America. The Model T was a triumph for mass production.

Other carmakers were quick to learn a lesson from Henry Ford. Soon, they too put assembly lines into their factories and

△ *Part-finished cars were rolled along the Ford assembly line, and new parts added as they reached various points. Here, the body of the car is being lowered on to the chassis.*

◁ *Henry Ford with the original Model T.*

began to compete with Ford's prices and reputation for reliability. By the 1950s, cars were becoming cheap enough for an increasing number of ordinary people to afford. Mass production turned a toy for the rich into an everyday means of transport for almost everyone.

THINKING MACHINES

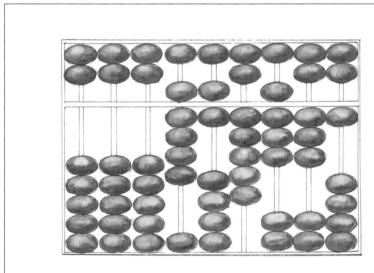

The invention that started as a way to make mathematics simpler has now developed into a vast network of machines used in almost every aspect of modern life.

For almost as long as people have been doing mathematical calculations, they have been looking for ways of making them easier to carry out. The task of adding up long lists of figures was no more appealing in ancient times than it is today, and there was always a danger of getting it wrong.

The earliest counting device was the abacus, invented in about 3000 BC, probably in Babylonia. In the simplest form of abacus, pebbles representing thousands, hundreds, tens and units were moved about in sand. The Romans had a version in which pebbles or beads were moved along slots in a metal plate. The modern abacus, in which beads are slid along wires in a frame, is still used in China, Japan, India and Russia.

The abacus was the ancestor of the calculator, but it only really helped by grouping pebbles, counters or beads so that they could be counted more easily.

△ *The abacus was first invented around 5,000 years ago, but is still used today.*

▷ *Early calculators: a version of the abacus (top); Napier's bones (centre); Blaise Pascal's mechanical calculator (bottom).*

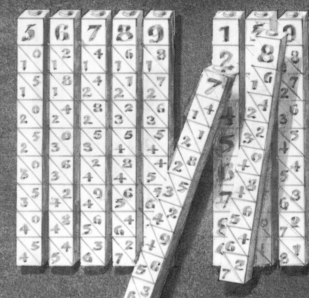

It did not do the work for you, as modern calculating machines do.

CALCULATING MACHINES

It was several centuries before anyone attempted to invent a machine which did this. In 1624, Wilhelm Schickard (1592–1635), a German professor at the University of Heidelberg, invented a machine which could add, subtract, multiply and divide. He called his invention a 'calculator clock'.

The first true calculating machine was made in 1642 by the French philosopher, Blaise Pascal (1623–62). Pascal was only 19 when he invented a machine to help

his father, who was a tax collector. The calculator, which he named the 'Pascaline', used a system of gears to add or subtract figures. It could tackle up to eight columns of figures at a time.

Later in the seventeenth century, the German mathematician Gottfried Leibnitz (1646–1716), invented a machine similar to Pascal's, which could also multiply and divide. Both machines used the same technique, known as 'single

▽ *Babbage's 'Analytical Engine' worked on a system of punched cards which were adapted from cards used to control coloured threads on a loom.*

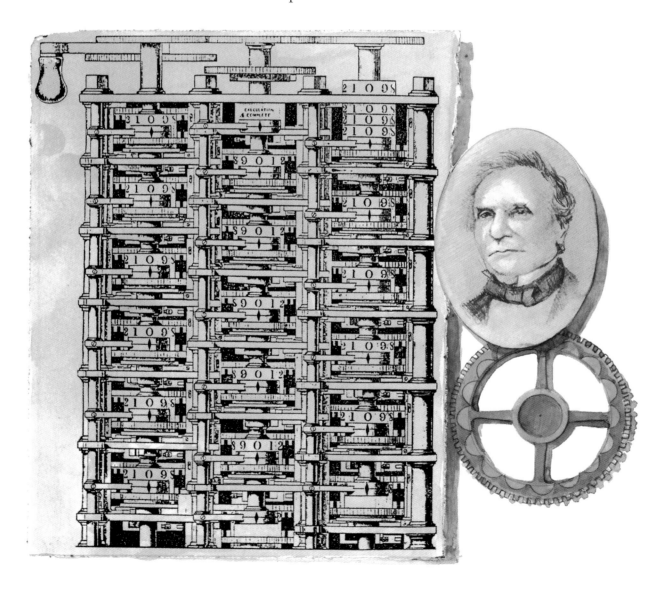

step' calculation. This repeats the same operation, such as a series of additions, to arrive at the correct answer.

People still needed devices to help them carry out complicated calculations such as long multiplication and long division. One mathematical aid was 'Napier's Bones', invented by the Scottish mathematician John Napier (1550–1617). This consisted of a set of metal rods with numbers on them. When the rods were lined up together in a certain way, they formed a multiplication table. Long multiplication calculations could be carried out by following the table and making some simple additions. Napier also invented 'logarithms' in 1617. This was a book of tables which converted multiplication to a series of additions, and division to a series of subtractions. By looking up the logarithms of numbers, and adding or subtracting them, even the most complicated calculations can be carried out quite simply.

△ *Ada, Countess of Lovelace, has been called the first computer programmer.*

THE ANCESTOR OF THE COMPUTER

These early devices were helpful but they did not begin to fulfil the work of the modern computer. The first machine to do this was invented by an Englishman, Charles Babbage (1792–1871). Babbage was Professor of Mathematics at Cambridge University when he began to experiment with computing machines.

His 'Analytical Engine', which he began to develop in 1835, carried out calculations and stored data and results. The data was fed into the machine on punched cards. These instruction cards, which were really early versions of computer programmes, were written by Babbage's colleague, Ada, Countess of Lovelace (1815–52).

The designs Babbage produced show similar features to the computer, although it was a mechanical rather than an electronic device. Lady Lovelace also realized that the machine would often have to carry out the same functions, and discovered a way of producing repeat instructions for the machine to follow, so that it was not necessary to punch cards with instructions that had been used before. The same principle is used in computer programming today.

Babbage never built a finished version of his machine, because he was always more interested in moving on to the next project than in completing a current one. Because he did not follow it through, few people knew about his machine, and it was many years before anyone began to delve into these theories again.

PIONEERS OF THE MODERN COMPUTER

In the mid-1930s, groups of people in Britain and the USA began to investigate the idea of developing a computer. In Britain, the mathematician Alan Turing (1912–54), published a paper describing a type of computer and the sort of problems it could work out. This paper was only theory, but Turing had the opportunity of putting his ideas into practice when he joined the British Intelligence Service during World War II. One of his tasks was to build a computer that would crack enemy codes.

Meanwhile, in the United States, Howard Aiken (1900–73), of Harvard University began work on an enormous calculator which he built with the help of the International Business Machines Corporation.

The work of these two men and their colleagues led to the introduction of the world's first true computers, the British Colossus and the American Automatic Sequence Controlled Calculator (ASCC). Both these machines were designed to carry out mathematical calculations much more quickly than a person could do them.

In fact, the rate of the calculations seems very slow by today's standards. The first ASCC could add two numbers together in 0.3 seconds, but this rate soon improved. By 1947, the Mark II model could perform the same task in only 200 milliseconds.

These early computers had many mechanical parts. The first electronic computer appeared in the USA in 1946. It was called the Electronic Numeric

△ *Alan Turing*

Integrator and Calculator, or ENIAC. The ENIAC could perform tasks far more quickly than the earlier machines, although it still used punched cards for data. This was a laborious process compared with today's method of using a keyboard and disks. Even so, in one day ENIAC was able to complete calculations that would take a human being a whole year to do.

▷ *The Fairchild computer circuit of 1961 was the first to be manufactured commercially. On the right is a short piece of punched paper tape which was used to enter data before the days of disks. Information had to be typed on to cards or paper tape where it appeared as a series of holes. The punched card or paper was then loaded into the reading part of the computer.*

PREPARING COMPUTER PROGRAMMES

A computer needs a memory or storage area where it keeps the data it is working on. It also needs to be told exactly how to do each task. Unlike the human brain, a computer cannot think for itself, so it has to be given very detailed instructions about everything it is asked to do. The set of instructions telling it how to do a particular task is called the 'programme'. Programmes stored on disks are known as computer 'software'. The computer equipment is called the 'hardware'.

Data is typed into the computer using a keyboard. The data appears on a screen or 'visual display unit' (VDU) linked to the keyboard, so the operator can keep a constant check for mistakes.

Information stored on disks can also be shown on the screen.

BINARY LOGIC

A computer processes information in the form of groups of binary numbers. In the binary system, there are only two digits, 0 and 1, and each number is made up of combinations of these two symbols. So 2 is written as 10, 3 as 11, 4 as 100, 5 as 101, and so on. This is ideal for computers because each symbol can be represented by the on or off position of electronic switches. An electrical pulse indicates 1, and no pulse indicates 0.

Binary logic was actually developed by an English logician, George Boole (1815–64), as early as 1859, and the ENIAC used binary numbers, but a series of lectures given in 1946 by the

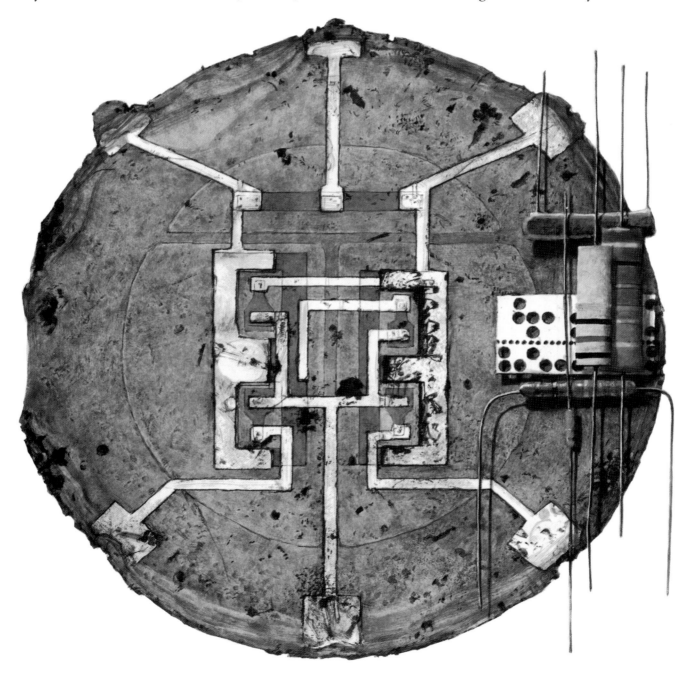

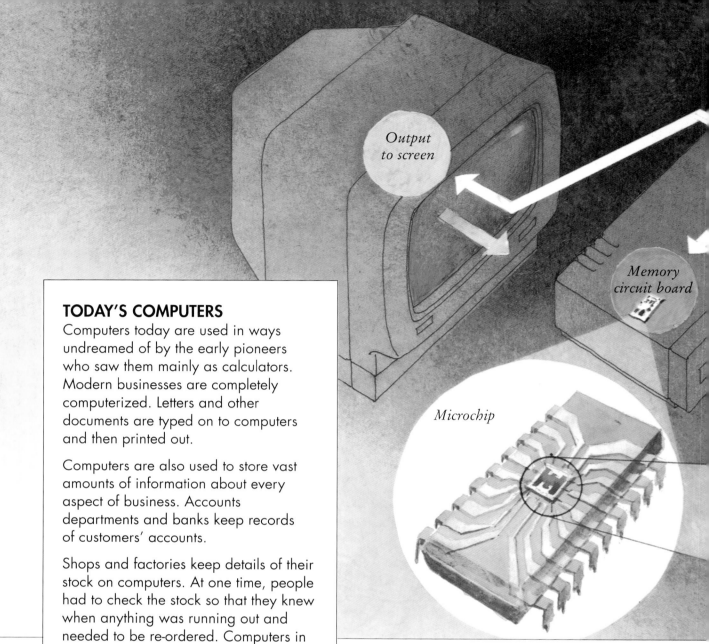

Output
to screen

Memory
circuit board

Microchip

TODAY'S COMPUTERS

Computers today are used in ways undreamed of by the early pioneers who saw them mainly as calculators. Modern businesses are completely computerized. Letters and other documents are typed on to computers and then printed out.

Computers are also used to store vast amounts of information about every aspect of business. Accounts departments and banks keep records of customers' accounts.

Shops and factories keep details of their stock on computers. At one time, people had to check the stock so that they knew when anything was running out and needed to be re-ordered. Computers in shop cash registers can now keep a record of every item that is bought, and send out an order automatically when stocks are running low.

Microchips are also used to give instructions to machines in less obvious ways, where there is no actual computer to be seen. For example, the robots which carry out work in factories are controlled by microchips. So are household appliances which can be programmed, such as washing machines, dishwashers and central heating systems.

American mathematician John von Neumann (1903–57) did a great deal to emphasise the importance of this system.

ON AND OFF

The binary system needed a large number of switching devices to turn the current on and off. In the early days, this was done by thousands of valves inside the computer. The valves used a great deal of electricity, and the machines got very hot. Computers also had to be very large and cumbersome to accommodate these valves. The next development was the transistor, which was introduced in 1948

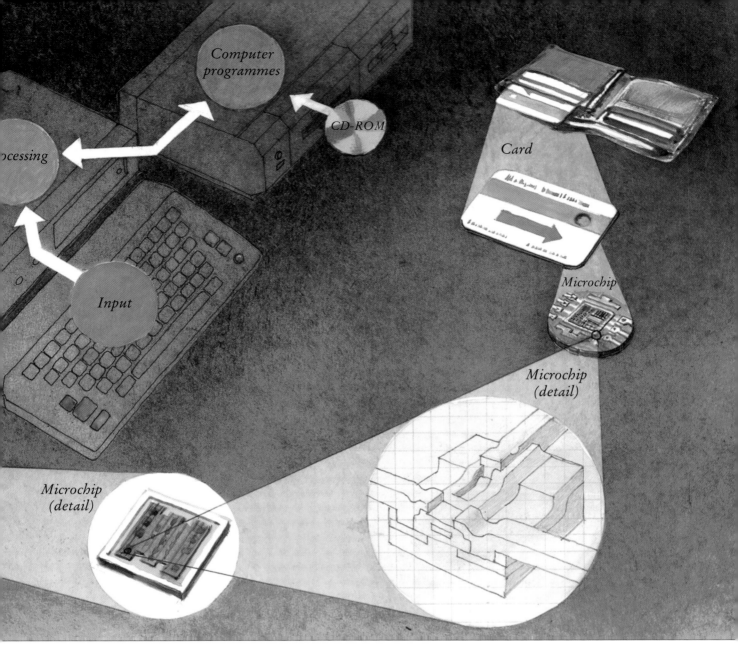

Computer programmes

CD-ROM

Card

Microchip

Microchip (detail)

Input

cessing

Microchip (detail)

by William Shockley (1910–89), and other scientists at the Bell Telephone Company. Transistors are lighter, stronger and more robust than valves. During the 1950s, they began to replace valves in all electronic equipment. The introduction of the transistor radio was one important development. Another was a smaller and more reliable computer.

SILICON CHIPS

Computers became even smaller in about 1964, when manufacturers discovered how to squeeze the components for different functions on to minute pieces,

△ *The first computers were huge machines that filled whole rooms or even whole buildings. Today, the same amount of information can be stored in a desk-top machine.*

or 'chips', of silicon. In the last twenty years or so, computers have become smaller, cheaper, faster and more efficient.

At one time, only governments or large businesses owned computers, but today many people have computers in their homes. The move to the computerized world we now live in has perhaps been one of the most dramatic developments in the history of inventions.

FIND OUT SOME MORE

After you have read about the ideas and inventions in this book, you may want to find out some more information about them. There are lots of books devoted to specific topics, such as trains or cars, so that you can discover more facts. All over Britain and Ireland, you can see historical sites and visit museums that contain historical artefacts that will tell you more about the subjects that interest you. The books, sites and museums listed below cover some of the most important topics in this book. They are just a start!

GENERAL INFORMATION

BOOKS
These books all present a large number of inventions of all different kinds:
Oxford Illustrated Encyclopedia of Invention and Technology edited by Sir Monty Finniston (Oxford University Press, 1992)
Usborne Illustrated Handbook of Invention and Discovery by Struan Reid (Usborne, 1986)
Invention by Lionel Bender (Dorling Kindersley, 1986)
The Way Things Work by David Macaulay (Dorling Kindersley, 1988)
Key Moments in Science and Technology by Keith Wicks (Hamlyn, 1999)
A History of Invention by Trevor I. Williams (Little Brown, 1999)

WEBSITE
For information on many different inventions, visit:
http://inventors.about.com

MUSEUMS
Many large museums contain interesting artefacts related to people of the past, and some have collections that may be more specifically about some of the themes covered in this book.

To find out more about the museums in your area, ask in your local library or tourist information office, or look in the telephone directory.

A useful guide is *Museums & Galleries in Great Britain & Ireland* (British Leisure Publications, East Grinstead) which tells you about over 1,300 places to visit. For a good introduction to the subjects covered in this book, visit:

Science Museum, Exhibition Road, London SW7
www.sciencemuseum.org.uk

For displays and information about many of the earliest ideas and inventions, go to:

British Museum, Great Russell Street, London WC1
www.britishmuseum.co.uk

WEBSITES
To find out more about the invention of the wheel, visit:
http://inventors.about.com/library/inventors/blwheel.htm

STEAM AND TRAINS

BOOKS
Hamlyn History of Trains by Colin Garratt (Hamlyn, 1998)

MUSEUMS
There are many train museums that you can visit, as well as old railway lines still running steam trains. Look in your local library or tourist information office. Some of the best museums include:
National Railway Museum, Leeman Road, York
www.nrm.org.uk
Birmingham Railway Museum, 670 Warwick Road, Tyseley, Birmingham
Didcot Railway Centre, Didcot, Oxfordshire
www.didcot railwaycentre.org.uk

Stephenson's *Rocket* is on show at the Science Museum, London (address above).

CARS

BOOKS
Car by Richard Sutton (Dorling Kindersley, 1990)

SITES
There are lots of vintage car rallies during the summer, when you can see old cars out on the road. Silverstone (Northants) and Brooklands (Surrey) racing circuits have regular race meetings for vintage and classic cars. Shelsey Walsh hill climb in Shropshire, among others, has regular veteran and vintage events.

MUSEUMS
There are many museums devoted to veteran and vintage cars around the country. These include:
National Motor Museum, Beaulieu, Hampshire
www.beaulieu.co.uk
Brooklands Museum, Brooklands Road, Weybridge, Surrey
www.brooklandsmuseum.com
Haynes Motor Museum, Sparkford, Somerset
www.haynesmotormuseum.com

INDEX

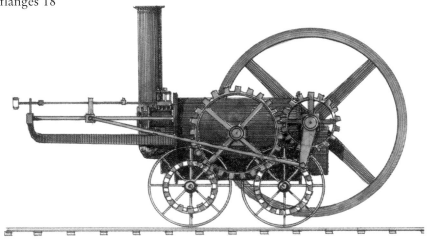

INDEX